YOU WILL NEVER SMOKE AGAIN

Discover an eye-opening approach to effortlessly and permanently break free from the enslavement of smoking.

G S Raman

DEDICATION

*To all the smokers who fell into
the trap and lost their lives.*

CONTENTS

INTRODUCTION

Every year millions of people try to give up smoking in the hopes of finally being free once and all from the addiction. Still, the majority of them fail. Why is that? What exactly are they doing wrong? Why aren't you able to do it?!

Like most smokers, you are unable to quit because you believe '*You lack willpower. You can't control yourself. You are flawed in some way. You have a highly addictive personality. It is incredibly difficult to quit smoking*'.

Many of the popular techniques people use to quit smoking are based on misconceptions about what smoking is and what it means to quit. The majority of us have been brainwashed regarding methods for quitting and this makes quitting far more difficult than it should be. So, how do you actually accomplish it?

As an ex-smoker myself, I am very much aware that *guilt* and *shame* won't help. I promise I will not make you feel guilty about smoking. The BEST and EFFECTIVE method to quit smoking is about learning to see smoking from a fresh psychological perspective and removing the desire to smoke in the first place by acknowledging that smoking has absolutely nothing good to offer.

When it comes to smoking, everyone has a different level of thinking and in order to quit smoking, it is important to understand how nicotine addiction truly works (physically and psychologically). Since the addiction process of nicotine is so subtle, many people do not fully understand how it keeps them trapped.

Combining my own experience with an accurate understanding of how nicotine functions, I have figured out exactly what happens to our body and mind when we smoke and what happens when we attempt to cut back on our nicotine intake.

Skepticism is natural for you because you are tired of failing again after trying every possible method, some of which are also highly expensive. A smoker's average success rate in quitting is only less than five percent. You may find it difficult to accept that a small book worth a few bucks will help you quit smoking. Putting myself in your position, I, too, would be skeptical. But don't let that stop you. There is a purpose for you to read this book: to earn the right to a healthy and joyful smoke-free life.

Before we delve deeper, let me clarify that I am not suggesting that you avoid friends who smoke, fear negative health outcomes, change the way you live, count the number of cigarettes smoked, experience shame or guilt, give up life's pleasures, use self-control to aggressively cut or quit smoking, or even use nicotine patches.

I'm simply going to modify your thinking about smoking, rewiring your brain and changing your relationship with cigarettes. Through examining the reasons behind your smoking addiction and exploring the misconceptions associated with it, you can effortlessly quit without experiencing any hardships or feeling like you're giving up something.

Prepare yourself for an innovative approach that will free you from the enslavement of smoking. Say goodbye to ineffective techniques and unlock your journey towards a happy smoke-free life.

As you progress through the book, you will feel ready and excited to quit, rather than feeling scared and anxious. Once you finish this book, you will never want to smoke a cigarette again, and you will have absolutely no cravings.

The book is divided into three parts. The first part talks about the reasons behind our smoking addiction. The second part deals with the obstacles to quitting. The third part teaches you how to become a happy and successful non-smoker.

NOW LET'S GET STARTED!

HOW TO READ
THIS BOOK?

Please follow these guidelines on how to read this book strictly, like an instruction manual, before moving on to the rest of the book.

Guideline 1: Do not *cherry-pick* and read.

This book is as short as it can possibly be. At times, you may want to skip ahead a paragraph or even a chapter. Do not do this. It will be similar to not taking half of your prescription and then claiming that the physician's suggestion was ineffective. So, please follow the book's chapter in order and refrain from skipping any section of the book, regardless of whether you find it to be repetitive. If something feels repeated, it is done intentionally.

Guideline 2: Don't *rush* through the sections.

Take your time with each chapter. Please be patient and do not anticipate being able to give up smoking until you have finished the book. Take a genuine interest in the book's approach. Determine for yourself the reality behind what the book states and how it relates to your own life. Give yourself enough time to reflect on the true knowledge presented in the chapters emotionally, mentally, and intellectually. If there is anything you don't understand, read it again.

Guideline 3: Avoid making *excuses* not to complete the book.

Our addiction and pre-existing beliefs about smoking cause us to postpone our quitting attempt. Be aware of your excuses ahead of time and eliminate them right away. Some of the justifications include:

"My life is very stressful now, I will read or finish the book afterwards and quit later. I have a special event /stressful situation coming up, I can't stop smoking before that".

Don't worry, I'm not telling you to stop smoking right now. I am only asking you to read the book. Just read the book, and it will take care of everything else for you.

Guideline 4: Do not *cut back* on smoking until you've finished reading this book.

Yes! You read it right! This book will prepare you to quit smoking. You are not expected to give up on the first chapter. Only at the end of the book will you transform into a non-smoker and quit smoking. For now, please continue smoking as you have been. I have dedicated an entire chapter in the final part of the book specifically on smoking your last cigarette. I can assure you that there won't be any withdrawal symptoms when you quit smoking after you finish this book. If you quit smoking before finishing this book, *then you will experience cravings.* It will cause chemical changes in your brain, reducing the psychological influence that this book has.

Guideline 5: Be *confident* and have self-belief.

Begin with a positive attitude. Making the decision to change your life is itself a wonderful beginning. Pat yourself on your back for making it here. If you can read around 50 pages easily, then you can easily quit smoking as well. Tell yourself loudly, *I am capable of quitting smoking easily.* You may find this stupid, but it increases confidence in one's abilities, making your quitting process incredibly strong.

PART 1

Why Do We Smoke?

CHAPTER 1

<u>12 Years A Slave</u>

I had a dream. Most of us are familiar with Martin Luther King's 'I Have a Dream' speech. I also had a dream one day. Except it was a nightmare. Except not one day, but daily. I used to have freaky nightmares daily, like cigarettes chasing me to death on a railway track near where I lived.

To be precise, I cannot even succeed in my "dream" to quit smoking. Nor did I want to. All I ever wanted was to cut down from smoking 2 packs a day to 2–3 cigarettes a day. I thought that would be my biggest achievement, and I aimed only for it.

I started smoking when I was 22, and I smoked for 12 years. I was a heavy smoker. I smoked 10–20 cigarettes a day. I got inspired and influenced by my mentor, and I started smoking with him. Initially, I thought one cigarette was not going to turn into a habit or an addiction.

I didn't think twice about smoking in the beginning because I thought cigarettes were cool and made people look grown-up and mature. Especially when you are in the creative industry, people will not believe you have creativity unless you chain smoke. After all, that's what I used to believe!

In my childhood, I always thought that people enjoyed smoking and it helped them relax. Surprisingly, I didn't like the taste of my first cigarette. As soon as the smoke entered my throat, I started coughing a lot. It tasted awful for a few minutes.

Because I was afraid my mentor would think I was "weak", I pretended it was fun. Aside from the thrill of experimenting something new, I didn't get any pleasure or high in smoking. It was a truly unfortunate experience.

Surrounded by fellow smokers, I continued to smoke occasionally. During this phase, the most common thoughts that came to my mind were:

'I can't possibly become dependent on it, it tastes so awful. I don't smoke frequently and I don't smoke by myself, It's just something fun to do once in a while. When I smoke, I feel mature and confident. Only other people get addicted, but I have strength; I am in control. When I become tired or experience a health issue, I will stop. Drugs and smoking are not the same. It is only drugs that are addictive. I can occasionally smoke without getting addicted'.

I can even manage to quit smoking for a few days or weeks at a time. And then all of a sudden, the number of cigarettes started to increase. Because everything takes place at such a slow pace, there is no visible change on a daily basis. At the start, I was able to go for a few days or weeks without smoking. Within the first four years, I began smoking more than ten cigarettes every day.

I was smoking with pride and passion. I would occasionally even smoke two cigarettes at once to look stylish and cool. I would smoke cigarettes when I was worried, when something interesting happened, or when I had a happy or sad thought. I smoked before a movie, after a movie, with coffee, with drinks, with every meal and in a variety of other settings. It was my reward. My partner in crime.

It boosted every single situation (or I thought so). Without awareness, cigarettes become a need rather than a choice.

Over the last few years, cigarettes have had such a negative impact on my life that I couldn't concentrate or focus without them. I couldn't even start the day without smoking. I was unable to engage in social activities without chain-smoking. My physical condition declined, the thrill of smoking faded as the years passed, and I experienced a range of health problems. I experienced daily episodes of coughing. My teeth turned yellow. My breath smelled bad, and I was in the worst shape.

Still, that wasn't enough for me to stop smoking. I found myself unable to quit, even though I knew smoking was bad and not healthy. I felt like I had been taken over by something incredibly powerful that held me and wouldn't let go! The problem was that I had no true knowledge or real understanding of what I was doing. It was like being in the bottom of a pit and having no idea how to get out.

My mind will come up with a new excuse to smoke and I also couldn't find the "right day" or the "right time" to quit. I will postpone my quitting to either tomorrow, next week, or next month, but definitely not today. Sometimes I would go without cigarettes for a few days, but I couldn't stop for long.

Without cigarettes, life simply wasn't the same and I always went back to it. I would have a hard day at work or see an old college friend. Suddenly all I could think about was smoking. I was not able to concentrate on anything and I would become irritated easily. And eventually, the withdrawal pangs would get to me to the point to just light up one cigarette. Before I knew it, I would be back to smoking one pack a day.

Being fed up with all the failures of my previous attempts, I made a new-year resolution in 2024 to quit smoking and be finally done with it. I developed a new approach for myself and it worked this time. I spent months studying books on addiction and behavioural psychology, viewing testimonials of ex-smokers and watching documentaries.

With my new-found knowledge, I started to understand the false beliefs associated with smoking. I realized how horrible the addiction was, as it had dominated my life for so long. I had a much better understanding of the addiction this time and it did the trick. I got my brain rewired to have no desire to smoke anymore. I was able to successfully quit smoking and became a non-smoker.

When I finally got off nicotine permanently, it felt like I had been in prison for twelve years and was finally free. It was an amazing feeling! I experienced an increase in strength, health, and happiness. I therefore stress that *anybody* can quit smoking, no matter whether you are a casual smoker or a chain smoker. This approach works for everyone.

CHAPTER 2
Baboon Salt Trap And Nicotine

A local bushman in Africa sets up what is known as the "Baboon Salt Trap" when he runs out of water.

Bushman digs a long, narrow hole and puts a lump of salt in it to set the trap. He does this since he knows baboons like salt. Baboons want the salt and put their hand in the hole to grab it. It's planned that the hole is just big enough for the monkey to fit its hand in, but not too big that it can't get its hand out of the hole.

The monkey could now open its hand, drop the salt, and run away. But baboons truly love salt and won't let it go, so it's stuck. The bushman can now catch the baboon. After that, the bushman puts the monkey in a cage or ties it up for a short time and gives it all the salt it wants. It is really thirsty because of the salt. The bushman lets the monkey go after some time, and it runs off.

Where does the monkey run first? It's the secret place where they know there is water. The bushman follows the monkey and drinks as much water as he needs.

Imagine that the Bushman is a cigarette company. The monkey is us. Salt is nicotine. The secret place is the bank, and water is our money. This is how we are trapped by cigarette companies.

We all know that tobacco leaves are used to make cigarettes and tobacco leaves contain nicotine. Tobacco plants produce nicotine to protect themselves from being eaten by insects. It is a built-in defence system that plants have had for millions of years. Nicotine is the fastest addictive drug in the world and people can become addicted to it after just one or two cigarettes. Within thirty minutes of smoking a cigarette, nicotine levels in the bloodstream drop to around half, and within an hour of finishing a cigarette, they drop to a quarter. This is the reason why most smokers smoke between 10-20 cigarettes a day.

If you inject the quantity of pure nicotine present in a pack of cigarettes directly into their veins, you will die immediately. To give cigarettes a flavour, tobacco companies also add urea to the tobacco leaves. In addition to the nicotine, tar, and carbon monoxide that you get from smoking a cigarette, you are effectively smoking urea. This makes cigarettes so harmful that long-term use can cause hundreds of bad health effects, including cancer and heart problems.

Before we begin to smoke, our bodies are complete. We then force nicotine into our bodies when smoking. When we put down the cigarette, the nicotine starts to leave our bodies. This is when we experience cravings and withdrawal pangs, which are just empty feelings that we often mistake for physical pain. We are not aware of what is happening nor we try to understand.

All we desperately want is a cigarette and once we light one, the craving goes away. We are now happy and relaxed, like we were before, when we were non-smokers. However, the relaxed state of mind is only temporary because, in order to get rid of the craving again, you will need to smoke more nicotine through lungs into the body and the cycle continues. It is a lifelong chain, impossible to break, *Unless You Choose To Break It.*
You may ask how nicotine turns smoking into an addiction?

This is how. Nicotine is transported to our brain through the bloodstream. Nicotine is absorbed by the brain within a few seconds of the initial consumption. After being absorbed by the brain, nicotine triggers the release of a neurochemical known as

Dopamine.

Dopamine is an essential chemical present in the brain. Dopamine's main job is to tell our brains which tasks are necessary for survival, like getting food and water, making friends, and having sex. It helps the brain learn, remember, and get motivated.

Our bodies release dopamine whenever we engage in activities, such as smoking. It provides a feeling of fulfillment or joy. For example, when you are extremely hungry and then eat food after a delay, you get a great sense of fulfilment or pleasure. That pleasure is the result of dopamine generation in the brain. Dopamine signals the brain that an activity like eating is vital for our lives and should be repeated again. It creates a strong memory in the brain, allowing us to remember to do this activity again when necessary.

Imagine what happens if we go without eating for a few hours? The dopamine levels in the brain eventually decrease. We recall from our memories that eating more food will make us feel better. This decreased dopamine level makes us feel hungry and serves as a motivation to eat more food, ensuring that we eat when we are hungry in order to survive.

Once we eat food, our dopamine levels increase, and we feel satisfied. The thought that food is essential to our survival gets stronger each time we eat. The cycle will continue for the rest of our lives. This dopamine loop prevents us from dying from starvation. It's nature's method of motivating us to do things we need to do in order to exist, such as eating and drinking water. Nicotine targets and enters this dopamine cycle. To summarize, nicotine has the power to absorb and control our mood and mind using the help of dopamine.

Whenever we smoke, we get a boost in dopamine levels. It puts an idea in the brain that smoking is enjoyable and essential to our survival, thereby causing our brain to remember and repeat this activity. The brain begins to believe that smoking is necessary for survival, much like eating. Each time we smoke, it establishes a strong memory of this incorrect belief that smoking is essential for living and encourages us to smoke again.

If you've smoked 2000 cigarettes in your life, for example, the false belief that smoking is enjoyable and you should do it again gets 2000 times stronger in your brain. As a result, nicotine has successfully seized control of our brain's dopamine system and is providing the wrong messages. In summary, nicotine has the ability to regulate our brain, which in turn influences our thoughts and feelings. This is how it traps you.

Tobacco companies, as well as governments, are aware of this addiction process. Making smoking illegal will not help the government in any way, as cigarette taxes generate huge revenue. Unlike other drugs, tobacco was so widely available because of this. Believe it or not, cigarettes really do kill more people than all the other drugs combined.

CHAPTER 3

<u>Driving Factors</u>

Smoking is more than just a habit. Habits are relatively easy to change. It is a *drug addiction*. By understanding the factors behind this addiction, you'll take your first steps toward quitting.

Although we can recall the moment or day when we decided to try our first cigarette, no smoker can recall the exact moment they "decided" to start smoking regularly. So, why do we smoke regularly?

Every smoker tried their first cigarette out of curiosity. Some found inspiration in their family, friends, or environment. We wanted to look confident, brave, strong, daring or cool. We just thought of "trying it once". Other smokers assured us that it would be enjoyable. They promised us that smoking can give us pleasure, a buzz, a kick, a high, etc. We were told it would be fun. We didn't want to miss out on this "fun". Who would!

We are not exactly what we were in our childhood. Our identity, values, and beliefs have changed. We were heavily influenced by the environment around us. Our brains form connections every time we see, hear, observe or read anything. These connections in our brains shape our thinking. These thoughts shape our wants and needs. The more repetitive the information is, the stronger the beliefs become, consciously and subconsciously.

The most pitiful thing about smoking is that the enjoyment that the smoker gets from a cigarette is the pleasure of trying to get back to the state of peace, calm, and confidence that his body had before he got addicted in the first place. How do you feel when your neighbour's burglar alarm goes off all day for a long time? Then all of a sudden, the noise stops, and that wonderful feeling of peace and calm is felt. While it isn't exactly peaceful, it is the end of the loud noise.

Apart from being a highly addictive drug, nicotine is also a powerful poison. When your body receives nicotine in response to a craving, you experience immediate relief and feel instantly better. However, this relief often leads to increased smoking, ultimately leading to chain smoking. But after two weeks of not smoking, 99 percent of the nicotine will have passed from your body and your physical addiction will be gone.

Why so then do we still relapse following this period?
The biggest issue is not nicotine addiction, but the *brainwashing* we are exposed to, whether it's through ads, the media, or family and friends who smoke. *It is the most important driving factor.*

The real challenge in breaking a smoking addiction is brainwashing. The struggle to "give up" smoking is something that almost everyone can relate to. But holding this belief is the same thing that makes it more difficult to stop. We light up when we're bored, anxious, or just want to relax. In contrast, smoking does not relieve boredom or promote relaxation. These concepts are the outcome of brainwashing only.

Smoking has no beneficial effects on relaxation or lowering your stress levels, despite popular belief. We smoke solely to satisfy our addictions and cravings. Our ideas of the benefits of smoking such as better focus and reduced boredom are nothing but illusions. We are fooled into thinking that smoking has its advantages. The fact that we can only concentrate on anything better after a smoke is because the thought of having a cigarette is itself so distracting, as you're not smoking now. Similarly, cigarettes do not alleviate boredom, but rather make you lethargic and hence more bored.

A lot of us think our lives are stressful, so it's easy to rationalize engaging in a bad habit as a means to relax. However, the majority of the stress that smokers go through is brought on by the discomforts associated with nicotine withdrawal. Smoking a cigarette will relieve this "stress", but keep in mind that people who don't smoke won't have to deal with stress in the first place.

The relaxed feeling we get after smoking only comes from satisfying your body's hunger for nicotine. We confuse the empty and insecure feeling arising from nicotine withdrawal, inseparable from hunger or normal stress, with physical pain. That is when we usually smoke, we think it's normal. In fact, many smokers no longer experience true relaxation anymore.

We have been heavily brainwashed from an early age to believe that smokers attain immense pleasure and a 'kick' from smoking. Our belief became stronger as we grew, as we noticed smokers spent a lot of money and smoked for longer periods of time. Why else would they do it if it doesn't give them pleasure?!

Smokers don't see smoking's true nature since it operates backwards. Because the process of getting hooked is subtle and gradual in the beginning, we don't blame the previous cigarette for that empty feeling when we're not smoking. When you light up, you get an almost immediate 'high' and feel less anxious or relaxed, removing that empty feeling, giving the lighted cigarette all the credit.

Now that the reasons for continuing to smoke have been shown to be false, what arguments are left to make us want to quit?
The chance to save money and get healthier are both good reasons. But these benefits don't happen right away; they happen over time. Since stopping won't make you feel young again right away, what can keep you going until you quit for good?! *The answer is the feeling of freedom.*

This insight will help you understand that smoking doesn't offer you any benefits at all. The real problem is our mental dependence on nicotine. The moment you realize this, you'll be on your way to finally quitting smoking for good.

CHAPTER 4

Loop Of Never Enough

It only takes a few seconds for the body to absorb nicotine. It quickly leaves the body too. Half of the nicotine leaves the body after around two hours. Therefore, our bodies' nicotine levels drop when we refrain from smoking for an extended period of time. Low levels of nicotine also lead to low levels of dopamine. We can't help but feel like something is missing or unsatisfied because of this. We call this feeling 'urge'.

Urge is like a bell that goes off to remind you to smoke the next cigarette. Our brains remember that smoking raises dopamine levels from previous smoking encounters. Consequently, we light up another cigarette, which increases the effects of nicotine and dopamine. To restore our nicotine levels, we are compelled to smoke.

This creates a cycle of nicotine addiction. For our brains, that's the key to being "happy and fulfilled". Due to not having true knowledge of our compulsion to repeat this addictive behaviour, we are not able to quit no matter how hard we try.

Every time we go through this cycle, the brain recalls smoking as enjoyable and forms memories of this occurrence. The memory gets stronger each time we do this cycle. Due to the fact that it exits the body so rapidly, nicotine is more addictive than any other drug. That means you need to get your next dose of nicotine in a very short period of time. Unless we take action to interrupt the cycle, it will continue for the rest of our life, just like the cycle of consuming food.

For some of us, the urge to smoke may be very strong and painful. But the urge is just a slight cue to stop and start again. There isn't much physical pain. If you sleep for eight hours, for example, your nicotine level is less than 10%. Right now, we should be going through the worst withdrawal symptoms. But when we woke up, we weren't in pain or suffering, right? Nobody is in such a lot of pain. We feel worried and anxious if we can't get a cigarette when we want one. It's hard for you to concentrate on anything. This feeling is not called Urge. The stress you're experiencing is entirely mental. "Craving" is the word for this kind of mental stress.

The human body responds to drugs physically by adjusting and modifying itself to counter their effect. One way the brain may adjust to a drug's effects is by changing the levels of certain chemicals called neurotransmitters. This adaptation causes the drug to lose the impact it once had shortly after first usage. The body has figured out how to withstand the drug's infiltration and yet keep its normal condition.

We term this thing "tolerance." When this happens, the original impact of the drugs becomes less potent, and more doses are required to provide the same effect. If you've ever used a substance that causes tolerance, you know that the user will keep taking more and more of the drug to get the same high. When someone suddenly stops using a drug they have learned to accept, an important effect can be seen.

The body is no longer balanced because it has become used to the drug and is now pushing against its effect, but there is no longer an effect of the drug to push against. We hardly even notice the gradual development of tolerance in our body.
One cigarette doesn't completely satisfy the craving over time, and the brain continues to crave more nicotine.

Consider the quantity of cigarettes you consumed throughout your initial year of smoking. At present, how many cigarettes do you smoke? How many more cigarettes will you need in ten years if you continue to smoke at this rate in order to feel normal? This is what tolerance has to offer. It occurs to every smoker. All smokers incline toward chain smoking because of this.

A significant effect of tolerance becomes apparent when a person suddenly stops taking the drug they are habituated to. The body is left in an unstable position since it is pushing back against the drug's effect because it has acclimated to it, yet the drug's effect is no longer there.

After eating, drinking, or engaging in enjoyable activities, we feel good or fulfilled, but eventually we return to our regular selves. This is how we live our lives. We are able to appreciate all of the natural activities in our lives repeatedly without growing tired of them. The first few cigarettes we smoke also have the same influence on our lives because nicotine modifies the dopamine system, which is in charge of giving us a pleasurable or satisfying experience.

Initially, smoking may be mildly enjoyable, and we feel good for a short time. But because nicotine is poison to our bodies, they fight back by making more nicotine receptors. After a few cigarettes, we start to develop tolerance towards smoking. As time goes on, smoking makes us less satisfied, and our desire for nicotine keeps growing.

We begin to feel Urge more often. We keep smoking more to try to get back to the amount of satisfaction we had before. So our brains fight back harder by making more nicotine receptors, which increases our tolerance.

At some point, we still don't feel as good as we did when we weren't smoking, even right after we smoke. We're now in the "red zone" of tolerance. Even right after smoking, our millions of nicotine receptors are still not pleased. We are NOT SATISFIED AT ALL. The amount of happiness and satisfaction we start with goes down. We smoke whenever we feel like it and feel a little better.

However, we still feel worse after smoking a cigarette than we did before we started smoking. Tolerance is the worst effect of nicotine abuse. Over time, your problem keeps getting worse. And it gets harder and harder to cut down on or control the number of cigarettes you smoke. You have no choice.

This addiction has dragged you down and made you less happy and satisfied with life in general. When you smoke a cigarette, you get rid of your urge and feel like you're having fun. You still feel worse than you did before you quit smoking, though. You have become more miserable all the time. The mood boost from nicotine, however, is only noticeable for about five minutes. You are stuck and blindfolded!

Let's say you have a rash that hurts. You feel like you can't stop itching and want to scratch. If you are not allowed to scratch, you become anxious, uncomfortable, and angry. When you really scratch the itching region, you only get comfort for a few seconds while you are doing it. The itching comes back after you stop scratching. It's very uncomfortable for you, like the URGE. You're once again unhappy.

Most of the time, it gets worse than it was before! Because the rash gets worse when you scratch it a lot. It works the same way for smoking. That's why we like our morning smoke more than other people do. Since you didn't smoke for 8 to 10 hours before you wake up, there is only less than 10% nicotine in your brain. When the nicotine level drops, the desire to refill the nicotine grows, and fulfilling that desire makes you feel better. It's as if the greater your hunger, the greater your pleasure from eating.

That's what smoking is: a lifelong itchy sensation, caused by the first cigarette you ever smoked. Smoking makes you feel normal for a little while, but it always makes you feel horrible. Neither the pain nor the pleasure would have been there if the rash hadn't been there to begin with.

Similarly, the uncomfortable feeling (URGE) is caused by the nicotine exiting the body. You lose the uncomfortable feeling when you light up again. Although you perceive it as happiness, pleasure, or relaxation, it is really just the uncomfortable feeling (URGE) being gone.

There wouldn't be any nicotine depletion If there was no nicotine in the system, which is the case for both non-smokers and you prior to smoking. Consequently, there wouldn't be any craving. This craving never occurs to non-smokers!

Addiction to smoking is similar to trying to itch for a quick fix while worsening the rash. Smoking never really brings you pleasure! The "pleasure" from smoking is nothing but a cycle of urge and removal of urge. I hope that you now fully understand this idea.

PART 2

Why Are We Unable To Quit Permanently?

CHAPTER 5

<u>Denial Of Addiction</u>

We don't say we have the habit of riding a bicycle or the habit of driving a car. We just say I ride a bicycle. I drive a car. Then why is it that we often say I have the "habit" of smoking?

Always keep in mind, though, that smoking is NOT a habit; it is a DRUG ADDICTION! We think we just "got into the habit" when we say we are "nicotine addicts." Thankfully, it's not hard to stop using nicotine, but admitting you're addicted is the first step.

Our stereotype about addicts is that they have miserable lives due to their drug usage. Either they're without a house or they're survivors of horrific circumstances. We didn't consider ourselves a "real addict" because we viewed addiction as a terrible thing to do. Addicts aren't inherently awful, and I wanted you to know that having a psychological addiction doesn't make anyone a horrible person.

We have to really train ourselves to deal with the cravings that arise when we start to smoke. In no time at all, we find ourselves unable to live without them and making frequent purchases. Anxiety sets in if we don't, and we wind up smoking more and more as we age.

This is due to the fact that, like any other drug, our bodies tend to develop a tolerance to nicotine over time, making it less effective, and hence leading us to consume more of it. Cigarettes no longer entirely alleviate withdrawal symptoms after a relatively short amount of time of smoking.

As a result, although lighting up a cigarette makes you feel better than before, you are actually more anxious and less relaxed than when you weren't smoking, even while you're smoking. This is even more absurd than putting on tight shoes just to take them off; after all, the pain gets worse with age, even when you take them off.

The position is even worse because, once the cigarette is extinguished, the nicotine rapidly begins to leave the body, which explains why, in stressful situations, the smoker tends to chain smoke. The truth is that smoking neither relieves boredom and stress nor promotes concentration and relaxation. It is all just an illusion.

From the point of view of the psychology of addiction, let's talk about some commonly held beliefs that are quickly revealed to be myths.

Belief-1: You Are Addicted To Cigarettes Because Cigarettes Are Addictive.

Rather than acknowledging that smoking addiction is an internal psychological process, this unacceptable statement implies that the object of addiction, the drug or activity, is what irresistibly draws you in. This is a highly incorrect belief that smokers believe very strongly which makes it difficult to quit.

Belief-2: I Will Stop When I Hit Bottom.

People with smoking addiction say this so often that it almost sounds true. However, it is a false belief that has disastrous consequences. "Hitting Bottom" is a meaningless idea. And it's bad for you. Most of the time, the idea that you have to hit rock bottom before you can really stop is just a way of saying that you should keep going until you've learnt your lesson is nothing but a carefully masked way to preach morality. Once you learn the psychology behind your addiction, there is no need to "hit bottom" in any sense, before taking control of your life.

Belief-3: If You Have An Addiction, You Are Self-Destructive.

A lot of people think that addicts' fundamental problem is their tendency to hurt themselves.. People with addictions, in their view, have an underlying issue with suicidal thoughts and behaviours. I think it's obvious by now that this idea is completely backward. When you feel helpless, an addiction is a strong response that tries to keep you in control of your emotions and your life.
The fact that they will almost certainly hurt themselves is just a terrible byproduct of the addictive mentality. One of these factors is that, similar to any other kind of addiction, smoking addiction too robs you of your ability to function and your sense of judgment. Immediate gratification of your compulsive desire to smoke takes position over longer-term considerations about what's best for your physical and mental well-being. That this frequently has undesirable side effects is hardly surprising.

Once you understand how addiction works, it's easy to see that someone isn't trying to hurt themselves, even if they aren't aware of it. It not only gives people self-destructive labels when they don't really have one, but also takes attention away from knowing what true addiction really is.

Belief-4: I'm Addicted To Smoking Because I Have An Addictive Personality.

Personality refers to an overall manner of adaptation to both the outer world and to one's inner feelings, and is a pervasive quality that defines much of who you are. People with smoking addictions have many kinds of personality. Only thing they all have in common is that they use an addiction to deal with their feelings. Confusing this with a whole "personality" has unfortunate effects. It mistakenly implies once more that those with addictions differ fundamentally from everyone else which is certainly a false belief.

Belief-5: Smoking Helps Me In Digestion.

One of the ridiculous beliefs smokers have about smoking is, it helps them go to the toilet in the morning. We can train our bodies to perform any task based on our needs. People who don't smoke have trained their bodies to go to the toilet when they wake up or after having a glass of warm water. Similarly you have trained your body to go to the toilet when you smoke. If smoking helped you go to the toilet in the morning, then why doesn't it do the same thing every time you smoke a cigarette in the noon and evening?

Smoking does not help but affects the digestive system in many ways. It develops acidity and increases bacterial infections. This damages the intestines and causes diarrhea. Psychological dependence may have influenced your perception of smoking's "advantage" on digestion. After quitting smoking, your intestinal health will improve and you'll lose this psychological dependence in days.

You might find it hard to believe that you were tricked into becoming addicted to smoking. Take your time to understand it. Think about why there are so many smokers in the world. Why do they continue smoking for what seems like an eternity? Why do sick people smoke even though their bodies are clearly telling them not to?

Is there something else in the world that kills so many people but is still consumed every day by more than a billion people? It is true that nicotine is a drug that is hard to stop using. No doubt about it, you have become hooked on smoking. It's also not your fault. At first, you only did it a few times because you were curious. Don't feel bad or guilty. *Keep moving forward.*

CHAPTER 6

<u>Cravings And The Fear Of Withdrawal Symptoms</u>

You can't just consume nicotine and then stop using it. A nicotine addiction can develop in anyone who regularly consumes nicotine, even if it's only once a week.

Quitting nicotine is simple once you know how, and even if you smoke once a week, you are going through the physical withdrawal process each week without realizing it.

The failure to address the psychological dependency of addiction is the root cause of your chain smoking. You keep going back for more because of this. The moment a cigarette is put out, the nicotine immediately starts to drain from the body, causing you to experience withdrawal symptoms.

Now is the time to debunk the myth that many smokers hold regarding the pain of withdrawal. When smokers attempt or are compelled to quit, they believe that the distressing physical and mental symptoms they experience are from withdrawal. In reality, they are primarily psychological; the smoker is experiencing a loss of his source of enjoyment or support.

The actual pangs of withdrawal from nicotine are so subtle that most smokers have lived and died without even realizing they are drug addicts. There is no physical pain in the body when you stop using nicotine. It is merely an empty, restless feeling, the feeling that something is missing.

This is why a lot of smokers think it has to do with their hands. If it lasts too long, the user feels anxious, uneasy, agitated, low on confidence, and irritable. It's like being hungry, but for a poison.

Nicotine does not directly cause withdrawal symptoms. We only feel the desire to smoke when our bodies don't have enough nicotine. Because the urge is so strong, we are more afraid of the withdrawal symptoms that everyone talks about. Those are all only in your head. They are nothing but psychological. We only face them if we quit using other methods.

With other methods, we experience cravings when we quit. Cravings are the mental sensations of anxiety and the sense of deprivation. These mental cravings lead our body to produce physical withdrawal symptoms including fever, anxiety, irritability, anger. You could be asking how physical symptoms could arise from mental cravings like worry, anxiety, etc. The answer is the concept of psychosomatic effects.

Physical symptoms or impacts we may observe and feel in our body resulting from our mental strain are known as psychosomatic effects. The concept is quite simple. You may have observed that your heart rate rises, your breathing gets faster, even your blood pressure rises when you are angry. Your anger is generating physical symptoms. And these sensations likewise go away when your anger passes.

For those with unresolved long-term anger, however, these physical consequences show up for months or even years leading to a variety of chronic health conditions. One could classify this as a psychosomatic condition.
For example, it has been proven that mental worry can lead to a lot of health problems, like high blood pressure, lung diseases, digestive problems, migraines, impotence, ulcers, and more.

Craving is a feeling that is a lot like stress and worry, and it can easily make us weak. It makes us feel physically ill, as if we have our hands tied behind our backs and must fight for our freedom at all times. These effects are thought to be the physical signs of nicotine withdrawal, but they are really the psychosomatic effects of cravings.

"I've seen people smoke two packs of cigarettes every day. They started smoking again after quitting, but now they only have two cigarettes a day". You might ask, how is it possible for them?

A big reason people smoke is that nicotine receptors in the brain never die. As a result, someone who smokes 20 cigarettes a day builds up millions of nicotine receptors. Their receptors are hungry for 20 cigarettes a day. Therefore, if they only smoke two cigarettes a day, they are constantly feeling a strong unsatisfied urge to smoke.

They are just having intense mental battles every day to keep themselves from smoking more. In their heads, they are always unhappy, miserable and never at peace, even if they can fight the urge. They have to convince themselves over and over again not to smoke. They are still getting urges every day multiple times.

For now, please don't let urges or cravings worry you at all. However, you should start to think about the good things that are coming. I'm so happy for you that you will soon find out how much fun life is without cigarettes. I promise you that you will have more energy, better taste food, no bad breath, more money, more self-confidence, more self-respect, and better sleep, better health and more time to fulfil your dreams. The list goes on and on.

Since smoking is a drug addiction, you can't stop without going through withdrawal for about a week while the nicotine leaves your body slowly. But this period is nothing to be afraid of. It is very mild, some don't even feel it. In fact, worrying about withdrawal is just another thing that makes it hard to quit smoking.

The first thing you need to do is fight the thoughts that are making you think that giving up smoking is a sacrifice. Many people make the mistake of thinking that they'll only experience a great change after a week of withdrawal, as if they'll experience some awakening and suddenly become a non-smoker. This is not true at all!

Your freedom begins not after your withdrawal period is over, but as soon as you smoke that last cigarette (as specifically said in the last chapter of the book).

CHAPTER 7

<u>Lack Of True Knowledge</u>

Dealing with an addiction without understanding its mental nature is like attempting to tame a tiger while blindfolded. Meaningful change is possible when you get to the bottom of your irrational decision to smoke and the underlying motivation that made smoking so appealing. Many smokers are really hard on themselves, constantly telling themselves they're stupid or worse for not being able to quit. It has been simple to assume that the only plausible reasons are a lack of strength or intelligence.

In order for an addiction to exist, one must have a psychological dependence, which is defined as an overwhelming need to engage in the addictive behaviour. On the other hand, some addicts consume a single physically addictive substance but never develop a significant physical dependence on it. This is the situation, for example, for those whose habit is to drink excessively.

No one would question that they are alcoholics if they drink to the point that it destroys their lives, but they might never drink for long enough to build up a tolerance that causes withdrawal symptoms when they cut back. Although they struggle with alcohol, they never develop a true addiction.

They were able to quit even though they were physically addicted because they did not have the mental addiction of addiction. Of course, physical dependence does make it harder to quit. It's also true that being physically addicted is neither required nor sufficient for being addicted.

People are afraid of going through physical withdrawal from drugs, especially if they think they will have to do it without medical help. This can make them more likely to keep using drugs. In the same way, physical urges can make it harder to stop. Having a physical addiction to drugs does not, however, play a part in the cause of true addiction.

Quitting is hard for many reasons, but physical addiction is just one of them. As with the large number of people who return to an addiction even years after being physically cut off from a drug, physical addiction does not play a big role in relapsing into addiction after a time of abstinence. Yet, it is relapse that is the real practical problem with addiction. Anyone who has an addiction has stopped at some point. As the old joke goes, "It's easy to quit, I've done it a hundred times."

But relapse is likely to happen if the mental issues that led to the addiction aren't dealt with. In fact, the psychological factors that lead to addiction and return are very similar. This is why examining the resurgence of cravings for an addictive behaviour can be so helpful in figuring out where an addiction comes from.

Some people don't believe that psychological factors cause addiction because they believe that saying something is psychological means it has to do with willpower, and they feel like they are being told they don't have enough willpower.

Sadly and ironically, people don't let themselves get relief from unwarranted self-blame that would come with understanding what makes them do addictive things when they reject a psychological theory because they see it as a test of their willpower.

You will have mastered your addiction and made it your tool instead of your master when you get the hang of it.

For some, the brain's need for nicotine can be a mild one, but for most addicts, this eventually turns into complete fear and the start of a very stressed out state of mind. Yes, the body is tense, which most people find uncomfortable. But how this affects the mind is very different for each person, which is why some people become hooked more quickly than others.

The smallest things in life can cause a lot of stress, and life is full of stressful events one after the other. The brain gets stuck in this pattern of behaviour, and they become scared very quickly. They'll soon be back to their nicotine sanctuary, usually when they're not as careful after having a drink or experiencing a very stressful day or event.

When you take in nicotine, your body goes into a calming state. Once your body is in a calming state, the conditioned response stops being activated, and the panic in your brain goes away. Experiencing that uncomfortable state again can be pure bliss if you've been in a big worry and are feeling very bad. Everyone who has ever used nicotine knows that sensation, and it's easy to mistake it for the actual hit they get from nicotine. It doesn't really hit you; all it did was make you feel better after being very uncomfortable in your mind and body.

You no longer fantasize about obtaining another dose after you've had one because, as your body begins to relax, your brain responds by ceasing to consume nicotine. The only time an addict's brain works normally is right after they take a nicotine dose. When you've had your fill of nicotine, it stops working and really tastes bad, so you cut back. When exposed to nicotine, the brain often responds in this way.

After a dose, you can think normally for a short time. If you really think about it, I think you'll agree that nicotine is no longer appealing to you, which is why you stop using it. It begins to taste unpleasant and if you keep consuming it eventually starts to taste pretty horrible. Naturally, addicts stop using drugs as soon as they feel "normal," and they rarely go beyond that.

Think about which cigarette is most important to you. Most

people will say the first cigarette in the morning, since that's the one that makes them least likely to want to smoke after not having any nicotine all night. Then, ask yourself which cigarette is the dirtiest. Most people will say it's the morning one, which is the same one. Now you realize that cigarettes don't give you anything besides help against your own addiction.

Quitting smoking is not a sacrifice or a matter of self-control. The real reason to stop smoking is to gain freedom. Finding the real reasons for your dependence on cigarettes and overcoming false beliefs about frightening withdrawal symptoms and decreased enjoyment of life will help you quit smoking with conviction and enjoy a new, smoke-free life.

Next time someone boasts about their self-control as if it is a good thing, feel pity on them. Because deep inside, they are dealing with a huge amount of unnecessary labour. But it's not their fault. Such is the ignorance around smoking. It's much better to break the false belief of smoking by understanding the reasons behind smoking addiction and feel good about yourself.

CHAPTER 8

<u>Using The False</u>
<u>Method To Quit</u>

We've all heard a lot of different ideas about how to quit smoking permanently. Most smokers will tell you it's a matter of willpower, or that it's all about realizing just how bad smoking is. Everyone who smokes made the choice to smoke their first cigarette, but they never chose to become regular smokers or never enjoy any occasions, like having a meal, without smoking before or after. Most people keep telling themselves they'll eventually quit, but they're afraid to actually do it.

Over 94% of people who try to quit fail. Therefore, 94% of smokers lack self-control. No, I do not believe so. A lot of smokers do well in other parts of their lives. Many successful people smoke. You need to be able to control yourself and be determined to succeed in any way.
Then what is it that makes smoking hard to quit?

Being able to control yourself does not have anything to do with being able to quit smoking. I know that the smokers aren't the issue. We are scared because we have failed in the past, but that was because we tried wrong methods, like self-control, quitting, nicotine replacements, and so on, and then we got "cravings." The easily available methods out there don't work and do not have the right tools to quit.

Using *Self-control* is the first method smokers try when they want to quit. In this method, smokers try to quit smoking by controlling their desire to smoke, relying on their will-power.

They make up their minds that they will not smoke again and that if they feel the urge, they will simply force themselves not to do it. They read about the negative health effects of smoking, hoping that it will reduce their desire to smoke. For a while, they get some success. They can hold back their urges for a few days or weeks.

But the Desire is always there. Then something happens. "A special occasion", "meeting a special friend" or "having a stressful event" when they think it's okay to have that "just one" cigarette. They smoke that one cigarette. Then another one. Maybe not immediately, but soon. Before they know it they are smoking everyday again.

Our brains are constantly using logic and reason to fight our cravings. One part of the brain that tells you not to smoke makes a list of all the bad things that happen when you smoke. The other part of the brain makes a list of all the good things about smoking and then says, "Smoke." It says that having one cigarette every once in a while is fine and that smoking is relaxing and beneficial for you. These two parts of the brain are at odds with each other.

When you have self-control, the first part of the brain wins the battle against the second part. But this fight never ends, tires us out, and makes us unhappy. We are trapped and angry. Finally, when the brain is worn out from fighting, we lose our willpower and choose to smoke one cigarette. And that one cigarette is all it takes to start smoking again.

Nicotine substitutes is the second way that smokers try to quit. This method basically tells us to use nicotine gums or patches to replace smoking. Please note that the main addictive part of the cigarette is nicotine.

It's only after a short time that we learn chewing gum isn't giving us the same pleasure and high as smoking, so we start using nicotine replacements and cigarettes together. The fact that we can't smoke makes us angry at some point. So we stop using nicotine substitutes.

It doesn't work because we want to smoke for more than just the nicotine hit. We want to smoke for the way it makes us feel, the test of smoking, the social aspect of smoking, having a cigarette in our hands and breathing out smoke. Nicotine replacement only takes the place of nicotine; it doesn't get rid of the urge to smoke. To say it again, it's very hard to stop smoking if we can't get rid of the urges and needs.

The third method is by *Cutting down* smoking. Cutting down is a lot like the self-control method. The two parts of our brain are always fighting until we can have our one (or many) cigarette of the day. It won't remove the cravings if we smoke fewer cigarettes. In fact, the more we try to fight the cravings, the stronger they get. It's like if I ask you to not to think of a particular song, the first thing that comes to your mind is the song.

In the same way, the more you try to resist the urge to smoke, the more you think about smoking. It makes you want to smoke more when you think about it. We've all been through this. You're not to blame. We've all tried to cut down on smoking, but it keeps getting worse. That's just the way our mind works.

There are thousands of articles and videos on the internet about how to stop smoking, as well as ads against smoking, family members and well-wishers making smokers feel like losers and forcing them to quit.
They do these things in the hopes that criticizing or forcing someone to quit will help them.

But they are completely useless and frustrating and make smokers less likely to quit. They make smokers feel guilty, which stresses them out, and because of that, they want to smoke even more. The last thing a smoker wants to hear is other people saying, "just quit it".

There are a lot of false beliefs and myths about smoking. This is the reason why more than 94% of quitting attempts using other methods fail. Each of those battles were fought in ignorance and darkness. That's why we should focus on knowing the truths about smoking. Not the scary health affects you already know, but the real facts.

The very important factor which makes quitting scary is the phase of misery that we expect will follow, when we won't be able to enjoy occasions like we used to, when we'll miss the benefits of smoking that we loved. Those who have tried to quit and failed are even more fearful.
But don't worry, once you transform into a non-smoker using the BEST and EFFECTIVE method, you will know that life without smoking is enjoyable, and you will get 100% confidence only when you actually go through life as a non-smoker and experience it yourself.

These repeated failures have real consequences on us. We are now convinced that quitting smoking is difficult due to the low success rates of these wrong methods. That we will not enjoy life as ex-smokers. And that we will probably fail if we try. This makes us procrastinate.

Our mind fools us with ideas like "I will quit later" or "I will try quitting tomorrow". Like we would for anything we find to be difficult. There is no reason to be afraid. Life without smoking was even more fun, social, relaxing, and cool.

Quitting smoking doesn't have to be miserable.
If you give up the right way you will stop thinking about smoking immediately. You will finally be able to beat this thing that has been controlling your every thought every day. Now you'll finally understand how your brain has been in a constant state of withdrawal ever since you started. Since then, it's been a never-ending fight to keep the pangs at bay. You will quit smoking once and for all, and you will get your life back. I promise, you will

never look back.

PART 3

How To Become A Happy Non-Smoker For Life?

CHAPTER 9

<u>No Gain No Pain</u>

It may be no surprise if some of you have read the title of this chapter wrongly as "No Pain No Gain." But it's the opposite. It is NO GAIN NO PAIN. It is simply a pun to remember that there is no gain in smoking, so there is no need to go through pain to smoke or to quit smoking. It is an easy way to remember that smoking cigarettes is not pleasurable or enjoyable; you are not gaining anything from smoking.

Sometimes it's very scary to think about giving up smoking. Many people who smoke don't even think about giving up because they know they need that regular hit. It is always ready to help you deal with any stressful scenario. It makes you feel peaceful and calms you down. You don't know exactly why, but when you go without smoking for a while you start to feel very uncomfortable. Gradually you begin to think about smoking and how good it would feel to have a puff.

There's a feeling of discomfort that gets worse the longer you go without smoking. When you're feeling bad, you can't stop thinking about smoking to feel better. You feel more and more uncomfortable as you put off your cravings, and finally the need to feel good again is so strong that you smoke one.

I remember many times driving around the city in the middle of the night to buy cigarettes and chain smoke on the side of the road to get a fix. Once you've had your cigarette, you feel good again for a while until gradually the whole process starts again.

It's a process that never ends. It takes over your whole life once you get hooked. Smoking now dominates every aspect of your life.

You've come to terms with the fact that it's just something you do. Sometimes, but not often, you might think you should stop, but something keeps pushing you forward. In fact, something keeps driving you so much that thinking about quitting can be just a passing thought and acting on it becomes very rare.

You may have tried to quit a few times early on in your addiction, but you quickly learned that it is very hard to just stop smoking. Without it, you just don't feel right. The more times you fail, the more likely you are to tell yourself that it's okay to smoke or that you will quit someday. The problem is that we can't control the future, and as time passes, we stop even considering quitting.

This is a trap that all smokers fall into. It's not really fun to smoke. The biggest scam in the world is nicotine addiction. That is not an exaggeration. Unlike other drugs that directly stimulate the pleasure areas in our brains, smoking doesn't give you a "high." Nicotine's high or pleasure is created by ourselves over time.

People who smoke don't really enjoy what they're doing. When nicotine is first used, there is no "hit." In reality, it's not enjoyable until you're addicted to it, which means you've used so much of it that your body begins to feel uncomfortable during withdrawal. No pleasure is felt until nicotine is used again, which eases the withdrawal symptoms.

As you go through withdrawal, you may feel uncomfortable. Using nicotine can help you feel comfortable again, and the change from being uncomfortable to comfortable can be very satisfying. That is the only hit nicotine gives you. It's like the relaxed feeling you get when you have to go to the bathroom but haven't been able to for a while, like on a long car ride. You get used to the uncomfortable feeling getting worse, but you learn to deal with it until you can get to a gas station.

Finally going to the bathroom can be very satisfying, and you realize how uncomfortable you've been. In a way, that's like being hooked on nicotine. The withdrawal symptoms of quitting nicotine are similar to those of a full bladder. The longer you refrain, the more pleasant your enjoyment of smoking will be when you return to it.

Do you now understand this most important fact about being addicted to nicotine? You could argue that this can't be true, but the truth is that all nicotine addicts have learned that nicotine makes them feel good because they have repeatedly felt uncomfortable and learned to connect nicotine with feeling better, or pleasure. They can't see it for what it is because it's so deeply ingrained in their minds. The withdrawal symptoms are very subtle when everyone first tries smoking; they can take or leave it.

Once the brain has become conditioned, it is really this easy to stop using nicotine. Remember the first time you smoked. It was awful, right? You didn't get high, you didn't get a pleasurable feeling and it probably made you feel sick.

All you did was wonder, Why on earth do people do this? No one has found smoking pleasant in their first try.
When people first try cigarettes, their bodies won't accept it. It is only when we are exposed to something over and over again, our perception changes and it starts to taste and smell good.

This is how the belief that smoking can help you relax first takes root in your mind. Because of this, the longer you smoke, the harder it is to quit, because your body stays tense even after you get through withdrawal. But that's only because it made you stressed in the first place. This is where most people go wrong as they fail to address this. This is how smokers get hooked on nicotine.

You are able to quit smoking the first few times you try, but you always fall back into the trap. It is only a matter of time before even attempting to quit becomes increasingly challenging. The best and most effective way to permanently quit smoking is to educate yourself that *Smoking is never pleasurable. You are not gaining anything from smoking.*

Think about how exciting it is to quit smoking. You will find more joy in every aspect of life. You will be able to do more interesting activities. You will be more productive at work. You can look forward to spending more quality time with your loved ones. You will save a lot of money which you can spend on whatever you want. Most of your health issues will disappear. Your confidence and courage will improve.

You will feel like you have more energy. Your heart and lungs will recover and you will be healthier. You won't get sick as often because your immune system will work better. Your mood will be better. You'll be happier, relaxed, calm and be less stressed. Your sense of taste and smell will improve. You will look younger.

Your sexual health will improve. The best part is, you will get freedom from the uncomfortable urge. You will finally be free.

CHAPTER 10

<u>Never Forget The</u>
<u>Law Of Nicotine</u>

Did you ever think about why we want to smoke even more when we're trying to quit? When we smoke less, the time between cigarettes gets longer, so our nicotine levels drop even more because we don't have nicotine for longer. As our nicotine levels drop, our urge increases. It's for this reason that smoking provides greater relief when cutting down.

We regard this as a state of pleasure. Compared to before, we're enjoying it more. Dopamine production results in more intense and vivid memories. That means the brain gets the message even stronger: remember, repeat. That makes us want to smoke even more.

Keep in mind that the need for more cigarettes is directly proportional to the number of cigarettes you smoke. The moment a cigarette is extinguished, the nicotine begins to exit the body and the brain's nicotine levels start to decrease.

The low nicotine levels created by the previous cigarette act as a trigger for the next cigarette. It works like a chain reaction. It's like if you knock over a domino, the next one will fall, which will make the next one fall, and so on.
This is the law of nicotine. Never forget this law. This law cannot be broken.

Let's look at what happens when a smoker smokes that "one

cigarette", even after giving up smoking for a long time.

He believes it is fine to smoke that one cigarette. What effects does smoking one cigarette after quitting have on our brains?

Most of our millions of nicotine receptors are reactivated by just one cigarette. Yes, smoking actually creates millions of these very, very tiny receptors in our brains over time. All those millions of receptors are still begging for more nicotine two hours after that single cigarette. Feelings of intense desire have returned.

Imagine that you used to smoke twenty cigarettes every day and then you quit suddenly. For some reason, you smoked just one cigarette after six months. The millions of receptors are reactivated immediately. You still have the tolerance that you built up earlier in your brain, fooling you into thinking that you can handle this occasional cigarette here and there.

Within a few days or weeks, you will be back to 20 cigarettes per day. Otherwise, you will have to deal with the uncomfortable urges. You'll be back in the red zone. Do not kid yourself into thinking that you will smoke just one cigarette once in a while. You'll never be satisfied with just "one cigarette."

All it takes is one slip to send you tumbling to the floor. If you haven't smoked in months or years, just one cigarette is enough to get you hooked again. It applies to all users, no matter who they are. This law is set in stone, but we can use what we've learned to stop smoking. It's not safe. You have to keep going down the slope until you reach the bottom.

You cannot quit nicotine if you keep consuming it, no matter how small the amounts are. It is important to stop using nicotine completely in order to successfully quit and return to normal life. This is the law of nicotine. No one can bypass this law. There is only one way to quit smoking permanently and that is to stop consuming nicotine altogether!

Everyone here knows someone who has tried to quit smoking and how grumpy they can be at first. This is because they are having a hard time controlling the panic that is building up in their thoughts. It is a constant battle in an addict's mind. It's like a wild monster and it needs to be fed regularly to keep it from getting angry. The more hungry it is, the more angry it gets.

Unless you stop using nicotine completely and get it out of your body, your brain will always be able to demand nicotine if you get "tense," which happens a lot in our hectic lives. This is why a lot of people who are able to quit for a while end up going back to it: they haven't dealt with the fundamental conditioning that has happened, which is the psychological dependence.

My life was ruined for twelve years, and when I finally got away, I felt like I had just been released from prison. Even though I've never been to prison, all of a sudden I felt free. Coming to terms with the fact that I had been hooked on the addictive drug, nicotine, every day for 12 years was a very emotional event.

As soon as things return to normal, you realize it was all a scam that has been ripping you off every day for as long as you've been a customer.

Once you get back to normal, you'll see smoking for what it is: the biggest scam in the world that has been ripping you off every day for as long as you've been a smoker. You'll feel calm and normal again, just like a non-smoker.

CHAPTER 11

<u>Motivating Yourself To Quit</u>

It may seem difficult to quit smoking once you're addicted to nicotine no matter how hard you try. So, millions of people who are addicted just accept that it will always be a part of their lives and stop trying to quit. No matter what, I promise that giving up smoking is the best thing that will ever happen to you. All of a sudden, you'll feel like the heaviest weight has been taken off of you. A weight you didn't know you were carrying. The realization that you have been tricked for a long time will hit you like a freight train.

Poor people are more likely to smoke than other people in our society. People see smoking as a cheap way to have fun in life instead of spending a lot of money on things like clothes, cars, houses, etc. We should start to think about why this is the case.

Why is a highly addictive drug, which does not have the expected hit effect, permitted to be legally supplied to consumers? Other than that it is another means of extracting money from us, it makes no logic. Smokers are absolutely conned every waking minute of their life by nicotine. We've been duped into thinking that nicotine genuinely has some benefit.. This drug only makes you feel good after it has made you feel bad.

There was no high when you first smoked. You didn't laugh or feel happy. After quitting nicotine for good, you won't want to use it again because it will make you sick if you do.

You've only come to this conclusion because you were made to believe it did something. It is because you saw other people do it in real life or on TV when you were younger. We're all constantly being hit with hidden messages, which is why you've been wondering what all the fuss is about until now.

There is a common belief that people choose to smoke, and it is up to them to decide whether or not they want to smoke. This statement is entirely false. The tobacco companies are well aware that the product they are providing is nothing more than a straightforward physiological trick; all they need to do is convince you to give it a shot. That is how powerful it is!

Keep in mind what you were like before you started smoking. You didn't need to smoke because you were happy with your daily life. You never thought about it. Can you remember that? That state of mind you had before you started smoking is what I want you to get back to, so please take some time to remember.

After quitting, your mind will be at ease again, and you'll start to enjoy life like you did before you became hooked. No longer will you need cigarettes to get through life. When you see other smokers, you won't feel tempted to smoke. Instead, you'll feel bad for them, which will be a nice reminder that you are finally free from nicotine. Most importantly, you will not feel like you are missing out on something.

Remember that smoking doesn't really give us a hit; it just lifts us from a bad state of mind to a normal one, which is what we think of as a hit. The only thing cigarettes do is make us feel fine. The uncomfortable urge can get so bad that it feels great when you can finally get rid of it.

By consuming nicotine, you give permission to the drug to make you feel bad when you don't use it, making you want to use it again. The longer the interval between the two cigarettes, the bigger this possible hit will seem.

A lot of the time, people who are thinking about quitting but haven't done it yet are just waiting for the right time. But when should you give up? When you're not so stressed? When don't you have to worry as much?

The truth is that there is no right time. The best time to quit is right now. It doesn't matter when you quit; if you do it the right way, you can do it at any time. Don't worry about gaining weight thinking that you will substitute sweets for cigarettes. Withdrawal pangs for nicotine may feel similar to hunger, but if you pay attention, you won't get them confused.
You just need to stop telling yourself the lie that "just one smoke" or a "special cigarette" is justified. Never forget that just one puff is enough to keep your nicotine addiction alive, and to feed the brainwashing that keeps you hooked again on cigarettes.

CHAPTER 12

<u>The Last Smoke</u>

Before you smoke the last cigarette, be confident that you will succeed in quitting smoking permanently this time. Really believe that you're about to accomplish something great. Read the book again If you have any doubts.

Always keep in mind that the nicotine trap is meant to keep you trapped for life. Make the positive choice that you are about to smoke your last cigarette. In a few days, nicotine won't be an issue, but some psychological triggers, like being in places where you connect smoking or seeing your friends smoke, might be. But you can get through it!

Never doubt your decision. The only things that make it hard to quit are the doubts and the waiting. Don't second-guess your choice; you know it's the right one. It will be impossible for you to win if you start to doubt it. If you want a cigarette but can't have one, you may be unhappy. But if you do have one, you will be even worse off.

Remember the real difference between people who smoke and people who don't. Non-smokers don't need or want to smoke. They don't crave cigarettes and don't have to use willpower to stay away from cigarettes. Which is exactly what you are seeking to accomplish, and you have every power you need to make it happen.

You don't have to wait to be a non-smoker or stop craving

cigarettes. You quit smoking when you put out the last cigarette and cut off the supply of nicotine to your body. YOU ARE ALREADY A HAPPY NON-SMOKER!

Don't resist thinking about smoking. If you do that, you'll want to smoke even more. Thoughtfully consider how smoking limits your freedom, and you'll understand why it's not worth the trouble to smoke. Giving up smoking doesn't mean you have to stay away from smokers or completely change your life. Have fun not smoking, be proud of your choice, and your life will make perfect sense now that you don't smoke.

Keep in mind that for a few days, your gut will have an unpleasant sensation that will try to stop you from smoking. You may only know how it feels to say, "I want a cigarette." During this time, don't use your willpower to fight the desire. Your body doesn't crave nicotine but your brain does. If you feel like smoking just "one cigarette" in the next few days, see that feeling for what it really is: an empty, insecure feeling that began with the first cigarette and gets worse with each one after that.

ONE LAST WARNING: DO NOT GET CAUGHT IN THIS TRAP! AGAIN! Make it a rule that you will never smoke again, no matter how long you have been smoke-free or how sure you are that you will never get hooked again. Don't give in to the millions of pounds that tobacco companies spend on ads; remember that they are pushing the most deadly drug and poison.

Remember, that first cigarette will do nothing for you. There will be no comforting withdrawal symptoms, and it is going to taste awful. It will give you nicotine, and there will be a voice in the back of your mind telling you, "You want another one". Following that, you will either be unhappy for a while or begin the dirty chain all over again. I REPEAT! DO NOT FALL INTO THE TRAP AGAIN!

You are now ready for your last smoke. Deeply breathe in as you smoke your last cigarette. You are already happy that you are not going to smoke. Consciously think about smoking your last cigarette as you smoke. Take a big breath in and ask yourself what it's giving you? Absolutely nothing!

When you put out the last cigarette, put it out with a sense of freedom. Don't think, "I must never smoke another" or "I'm not allowed to smoke another."

Instead, think, ISN'T IT GREAT! I'M FREE! I'M NOT A SLAVE TO THIS NICOTINE ANYMORE! I will never again have to put these disgusting things in my mouth.

Embrace Yourself For The Greatest Thing You Are Going To Accomplish! Never Doubt Your Decision! Strongly Believe That You Are Already A Happy Non-Smoker!

Good luck, buddy. Happy quitting.

Printed in Great Britain
by Amazon

47479753R00036